CONTENTS

HORSE INFORMATION

"No philosophers so thoroughly
comprehend us as dogs and horses."
HERMAN MELVILLE

Name				
Age	Height	Sex	Weight	Date of Ownership
Breed			Breed Registration Number	
Colour and Markings		Temperature	Pulse	Respiration Rate
Veterinarian Name and Contact Information				
Farrier Name and Contact Information				
Trainer Name and Contact Information				
Hay (lbs or Flakes Per Day)		Feed Type and Amount Per Day		
Supplement Type(s) and Amount(s) Per Day		Medications(s) and Amount(s) Per Day		
Turnout Schedule		Notes		

Name				
Age	Height	Sex	Weight	Date of Ownership
Breed			Breed Registration Number	
Colour and Markings		Temperature	Pulse	Respiration Rate
Veterinarian Name and Contact Information				
Farrier Name and Contact Information				
Trainer Name and Contact Information				
Hay (lbs or Flakes Per Day)			Feed Type and Amount Per Day	
Supplement Type(s) and Amount(s) Per Day			Medications(s) and Amount(s) Per Day	
Turnout Schedule			Notes	

Name				

Age	Height	Sex	Weight	Date of Ownership

Breed	Breed Registration Number

Colour and Markings	Temperature	Pulse	Respiration Rate

Veterinarian Name and Contact Information

Farrier Name and Contact Information

Trainer Name and Contact Information

Hay (lbs or Flakes Per Day)	Feed Type and Amount Per Day

Supplement Type(s) and Amount(s) Per Day	Medications(s) and Amount(s) Per Day

Turnout Schedule	Notes

Name				
Age	Height	Sex	Weight	Date of Ownership

Breed	Breed Registration Number

Colour and Markings	Temperature	Pulse	Respiration Rate

Veterinarian Name and Contact Information

Farrier Name and Contact Information

Trainer Name and Contact Information

Hay (lbs or Flakes Per Day)	Feed Type and Amount Per Day

Supplement Type(s) and Amount(s) Per Day	Medications(s) and Amount(s) Per Day

Turnout Schedule	Notes

HORSE HEALTH

"If anybody expects to calm a horse down by
tiring him out with riding swiftly and far, his
supposition is the reverse of the truth."
XENOPHON

Signs of Good Health

An average horse at rest will have the following vital signs (individual horses will vary, so it's important to check what's normal for your horse):

Temperature: Approximately 38ºC
Pulse: Between 28 and 40 Beats per Minute
Respiration: Between 8 to 16 Breaths per Minute

Other signs of good health include:

☐ Clear and Regular Heartbeat	☐ Soft, Smooth and Shiny Coat
☐ Quiet and Regular Breaths, Especially at Rest	☐ Good Appetite
☐ Clear, Alert Eyes	☐ Light and Regular Gut Sounds
☐ Relaxed Ears	☐ Firm Droppings
☐ Clean Nose (a little clear discharge is normal)	☐ Legs Free of Heat, Pain and Swelling
☐ Moist, Pink Gums	☐ Elastic Skin
☐ Quick Capillary Refill Time (less than 2 seconds if the gums are pressed with a thumb)	☐ Adequate Water Consumption (25-55 Liters of Water/Day)
☐ Willingness to Move Forward in Hand and Under Saddle	☐ Good Body Condition (a general rule for optimal body condition is to be able to feel the horse's ribs, but not see them)

Things To Look Out For

The following conditions may indicate a health or lameness issue, especially if they come on suddenly:

☐ Unusual or Extreme Mood Changes	☐ Discomfort While Eating, Spilling Food
☐ Lethargy, Disinterest	☐ Reluctance to Drink
☐ Shallow, Quick, Irregular or Laboured Breathing	☐ Dry, Pale Gums
☐ Rapid, Shallow Heartbeat	☐ Swollen Lymph Nodes
☐ Fever	☐ Thick Nasal Discharge
☐ Slow Capillary Refill Time (more than 2 seconds if the gums are pressed with a thumb)	☐ Cloudy, Congested, Runny, Squinting, Painful, Sunken or Swollen Eyes
☐ Changes in Appetite	☐ Sudden Changes in Body Condition
☐ Discomfort and Distress (can include excessive pawing, rolling, kicking out, elevated respiration rate)	☐ Dehydration (skin doesn't immediately spring back if gently pulled)
☐ Dull, Dry Flaky Coat	☐ Any Unusual or Sudden Swellings
☐ Discoloured Urine or Difficulty Urinating	☐ Heat, Pain or Swelling of Any Part of a Limb
☐ Loose Droppings or Difficulty Passing Droppings	☐ Unusual Reluctance to Move Forward
☐ Stiffness or Short-Stridedness	☐ Reluctance to Perform Regular Tasks
☐ Long, Brittle, Cracked or Crumbling Hooves	

"A canter is a cure for every evil."
BENJAMIN DISRAELI

ROUTINE CARE

"Care, and not fine stables, makes a good horse."
DANISH PROVERB

Vaccinations

DATES	DESCRIPTION

Worming

DATES	DESCRIPTION

Dental Work

DATES	DESCRIPTION

Feed Changes

DATES	DESCRIPTION

Supplement Changes

DATES	DESCRIPTION

Medicine Changes

DATES	DESCRIPTION

Turnout Changes

DATES	DESCRIPTION

Shoeing Changes

DATES	DESCRIPTION

Saddle Fit

DATES	DESCRIPTION

Chiropractic Work

DATES	DESCRIPTION

Massage Work

DATES	DESCRIPTION

Joint Injections

DATES	DESCRIPTION

Other Maintenance

DATES	DESCRIPTION

Lameness History

DATE	DESCRIPTION	TREATMENT	OUTCOME

Record of Farrier Visits

DATE	WORK DONE	NOTES / RECOMMENDATIONS

Record of Vet Visits

DATE	WORK DONE	NOTES / RECOMMENDATIONS

TRAINING GOALS
AND WEEKLY PLANNER

"Grooming: the process by which the dirt on
the horse is transferred to the groom"

Weekly Goals

DATE: _____

_____

_____

_____

_____

MONDAY
TUESDAY
WEDNESDAY
THURSDAY
FRIDAY
SATURDAY
SUNDAY

"It's always been and always will be the same in the world:
The horse does the work and the coachman is tipped."

DATE: _____ # Weekly Goals

_____
_____
_____
_____

MONDAY
TUESDAY
WEDNESDAY
THURSDAY
FRIDAY
SATURDAY
SUNDAY

DATE: _____ # Weekly Goals

_____

_____

_____

_____

| **MONDAY** |
| **TUESDAY** |
| **WEDNESDAY** |
| **THURSDAY** |
| **FRIDAY** |
| **SATURDAY** |
| **SUNDAY** |

"The ass will carry his load, but not a double load; ride
not a free horse to death." - Miguel de Cervantes

DATE: _____   # Weekly Goals

_____

_____

_____

_____

MONDAY	
TUESDAY	
WEDNESDAY	
THURSDAY	
FRIDAY	
SATURDAY	
SUNDAY	

DATE: _____

Weekly Goals

_____

_____

_____

_____

MONDAY
TUESDAY
WEDNESDAY
THURSDAY
FRIDAY
SATURDAY
SUNDAY

"There is just as much horse sense as ever, but the horses have most of it."

DATE: _____ # Weekly Goals

_____

_____

_____

_____

MONDAY
TUESDAY
WEDNESDAY
THURSDAY
FRIDAY
SATURDAY
SUNDAY

Weekly Goals

_____

_____

_____

_____

MONDAY	
TUESDAY	
WEDNESDAY	
THURSDAY	
FRIDAY	
SATURDAY	
SUNDAY	

"Riding a horse is not a gentle hobby, to be picked up and laid down
like a game of Solitaire. It is a grand passion." - Ralph Waldo Emerson

DATE: _____   # Weekly Goals

_____

_____

_____

_____

MONDAY	
TUESDAY	
WEDNESDAY	
THURSDAY	
FRIDAY	
SATURDAY	
SUNDAY	

Weekly Goals

_____

_____

_____

_____

MONDAY	
TUESDAY	
WEDNESDAY	
THURSDAY	
FRIDAY	
SATURDAY	
SUNDAY	

"If your horse says no, you either asked the wrong
question, or asked the question wrong." - Pat Parelli

DATE: _____ # Weekly Goals

_____

_____

_____

_____

MONDAY
TUESDAY
WEDNESDAY
THURSDAY
FRIDAY
SATURDAY
SUNDAY

DATE: _____ # Weekly Goals

_____

_____

_____

_____

MONDAY
TUESDAY
WEDNESDAY
THURSDAY
FRIDAY
SATURDAY
SUNDAY

"A Horseman should know neither fear, nor anger." - James Rarey

DATE: _____   # Weekly Goals

_____

_____

_____

_____

MONDAY	
TUESDAY	
WEDNESDAY	
THURSDAY	
FRIDAY	
SATURDAY	
SUNDAY	

DATE: _____   # Weekly Goals

_____

_____

_____

_____

MONDAY	
TUESDAY	
WEDNESDAY	
THURSDAY	
FRIDAY	
SATURDAY	
SUNDAY	

"The daughter who won't lift a finger in the house is the same child who cycles madly off
in the pouring rain to spend all morning mucking out a stable." - Samantha Armstrong

Weekly Goals

_____

_____

_____

_____

MONDAY
TUESDAY
WEDNESDAY
THURSDAY
FRIDAY
SATURDAY
SUNDAY

DATE: _____ # Weekly Goals

_____
_____
_____
_____

MONDAY	
TUESDAY	
WEDNESDAY	
THURSDAY	
FRIDAY	
SATURDAY	
SUNDAY	

"I've spent most of my life riding horses. The rest I've just wasted."

DATE: _____ # Weekly Goals

_____

_____

_____

_____

MONDAY
TUESDAY
WEDNESDAY
THURSDAY
FRIDAY
SATURDAY
SUNDAY

DATE: _____ # Weekly Goals

_____

_____

_____

_____

MONDAY
TUESDAY
WEDNESDAY
THURSDAY
FRIDAY
SATURDAY
SUNDAY

"If you act like you've only got fifteen minutes, it'll take all day. Act like
you've got all day and it'll take fifteen minutes." - Monty Roberts

DATE: _____   # Weekly Goals

_____

_____

_____

_____

| **MONDAY** |
| **TUESDAY** |
| **WEDNESDAY** |
| **THURSDAY** |
| **FRIDAY** |
| **SATURDAY** |
| **SUNDAY** |

DATE: _____ # Weekly Goals

_____
_____
_____
_____

MONDAY
TUESDAY
WEDNESDAY
THURSDAY
FRIDAY
SATURDAY
SUNDAY

"Whoever said a horse was dumb, was dumb." - Will Rogers

DATE: _____   # Weekly Goals

_____
_____
_____
_____

MONDAY
TUESDAY
WEDNESDAY
THURSDAY
FRIDAY
SATURDAY
SUNDAY

DATE: _____ # Weekly Goals

_____

_____

_____

_____

MONDAY
TUESDAY
WEDNESDAY
THURSDAY
FRIDAY
SATURDAY
SUNDAY

"One who believes that he has mastered the art of horsemanship has not yet begun to understand the horse."

DATE: _____   # Weekly Goals

_____

_____

_____

_____

MONDAY
TUESDAY
WEDNESDAY
THURSDAY
FRIDAY
SATURDAY
SUNDAY

Weekly Goals

_____

_____

_____

_____

MONDAY	
TUESDAY	
WEDNESDAY	
THURSDAY	
FRIDAY	
SATURDAY	
SUNDAY	

"The horse you get off is not the same as the horse you got on. It is your job
as a rider to ensure that as often as possible, the change is for the better."

DATE: _____ # Weekly Goals

_____

_____

_____

_____

MONDAY
TUESDAY
WEDNESDAY
THURSDAY
FRIDAY
SATURDAY
SUNDAY

DATE: _____

Weekly Goals

_____

_____

_____

_____

MONDAY	
TUESDAY	
WEDNESDAY	
THURSDAY	
FRIDAY	
SATURDAY	
SUNDAY	

"If a horse becomes more beautiful in the course of his work, it is a
sign that the training principles are correct." - Colonel Podhajsky

DATE: _____   # Weekly Goals

_____
_____
_____
_____

MONDAY
TUESDAY
WEDNESDAY
THURSDAY
FRIDAY
SATURDAY
SUNDAY

DATE: _____

Weekly Goals

_____

_____

_____

_____

MONDAY
TUESDAY
WEDNESDAY
THURSDAY
FRIDAY
SATURDAY
SUNDAY

"There are only two emotions that belong in the saddle; one is
a sense of humor and the other is patience." - John Lyons

DATE: _____   # Weekly Goals

_____

_____

_____

_____

| MONDAY |
| TUESDAY |
| WEDNESDAY |
| THURSDAY |
| FRIDAY |
| SATURDAY |
| SUNDAY |

DATE: _____   # Weekly Goals

_____

_____

_____

_____

MONDAY	
TUESDAY	
WEDNESDAY	
THURSDAY	
FRIDAY	
SATURDAY	
SUNDAY	

"You cannot train a horse with shouts and expect it to obey a whisper. " - Dagobert D. Runes

DATE: _____ # Weekly Goals

_____
_____
_____
_____

MONDAY	
TUESDAY	
WEDNESDAY	
THURSDAY	
FRIDAY	
SATURDAY	
SUNDAY	

DATE: _____ # Weekly Goals

_____
_____
_____
_____

MONDAY	
TUESDAY	
WEDNESDAY	
THURSDAY	
FRIDAY	
SATURDAY	
SUNDAY	

"Correction does much for the horse, but encouragement does more."

DATE: _____ # Weekly Goals

_____
_____
_____
_____

MONDAY
TUESDAY
WEDNESDAY
THURSDAY
FRIDAY
SATURDAY
SUNDAY

DATE: _____   # Weekly Goals

_____

_____

_____

_____

MONDAY

TUESDAY

WEDNESDAY

THURSDAY

FRIDAY

SATURDAY

SUNDAY

"Horse sense is the thing a horse has which keeps it from betting on people." – W.C. Fields

DATE: _____ # Weekly Goals

_____

_____

_____

_____

MONDAY	
TUESDAY	
WEDNESDAY	
THURSDAY	
FRIDAY	
SATURDAY	
SUNDAY	

DATE: _____   # Weekly Goals

_____

_____

_____

_____

MONDAY	
TUESDAY	
WEDNESDAY	
THURSDAY	
FRIDAY	
SATURDAY	
SUNDAY	

"When in doubt, ask a horse."

DATE: _____   # Weekly Goals

_____

_____

_____

_____

MONDAY	
TUESDAY	
WEDNESDAY	
THURSDAY	
FRIDAY	
SATURDAY	
SUNDAY	

DATE: _____   # Weekly Goals

_____

_____

_____

_____

MONDAY
TUESDAY
WEDNESDAY
THURSDAY
FRIDAY
SATURDAY
SUNDAY

"In training horses, one trains himself." - Antoine De Pluvinet

DATE: _____ # Weekly Goals

_____

_____

_____

_____

MONDAY

TUESDAY

WEDNESDAY

THURSDAY

FRIDAY

SATURDAY

SUNDAY

Weekly Goals

_____

_____

_____

_____

MONDAY	
TUESDAY	
WEDNESDAY	
THURSDAY	
FRIDAY	
SATURDAY	
SUNDAY	

"When riding my horse I no longer have my heart in my chest, but between my knees."

DATE: _____   # Weekly Goals

_____

_____

_____

_____

| **MONDAY** |
| **TUESDAY** |
| **WEDNESDAY** |
| **THURSDAY** |
| **FRIDAY** |
| **SATURDAY** |
| **SUNDAY** |

Weekly Goals

_____

_____

_____

_____

MONDAY	
TUESDAY	
WEDNESDAY	
THURSDAY	
FRIDAY	
SATURDAY	
SUNDAY	

"A horse is like a violin, first it must be tuned, and when tuned it must be accurately played."

DATE: _____ # Weekly Goals

_____

_____

_____

_____

MONDAY
TUESDAY
WEDNESDAY
THURSDAY
FRIDAY
SATURDAY
SUNDAY

DATE: _____ # **Weekly Goals**

_____

_____

_____

_____

MONDAY
TUESDAY
WEDNESDAY
THURSDAY
FRIDAY
SATURDAY
SUNDAY

"A stubborn horse walks behind you, an impatient horse walks
in front of you, but a noble companion walks beside you."

DATE: _____ # Weekly Goals

_____

_____

_____

_____

MONDAY
TUESDAY
WEDNESDAY
THURSDAY
FRIDAY
SATURDAY
SUNDAY

DATE: _____

Weekly Goals

_____

_____

_____

_____

MONDAY
TUESDAY
WEDNESDAY
THURSDAY
FRIDAY
SATURDAY
SUNDAY

"A horse loves freedom, and the weariest old work horse will roll on the ground or break into a lumbering gallop when he is turned loose into the open." - Gerald Raferty

Weekly Goals

DATE: _____

_____

_____

_____

_____

MONDAY
TUESDAY
WEDNESDAY
THURSDAY
FRIDAY
SATURDAY
SUNDAY

DATE: _____

Weekly Goals

_____

_____

_____

_____

MONDAY
TUESDAY
WEDNESDAY
THURSDAY
FRIDAY
SATURDAY
SUNDAY

"I whisper to my horse, but he never listens!"

DATE: _____ # Weekly Goals

_____

_____

_____

_____

MONDAY	
TUESDAY	
WEDNESDAY	
THURSDAY	
FRIDAY	
SATURDAY	
SUNDAY	

DATE: _____ # Weekly Goals

_____

_____

_____

_____

MONDAY
TUESDAY
WEDNESDAY
THURSDAY
FRIDAY
SATURDAY
SUNDAY

"Of all creatures God made at the Creation, there is none more excellent,
or so much to be respected as a horse." - Bedouin Legend

Weekly Goals

_____

_____

_____

_____

MONDAY	
TUESDAY	
WEDNESDAY	
THURSDAY	
FRIDAY	
SATURDAY	
SUNDAY	

DATE: _____

Weekly Goals

_____
_____
_____
_____

MONDAY	
TUESDAY	
WEDNESDAY	
THURSDAY	
FRIDAY	
SATURDAY	
SUNDAY	

"The hardest thing about learning to ride is the ground!"

SHOWS

"No hour of life is wasted
that is spent in the saddle."
WINSTON CHURCHILL

Show Checklist

FOR THE HORSE

- ☐ Equine First Aid Kit
- ☐ Hay and Hay Net
- ☐ Water Buckets, Clips and Jugs of Water
- ☐ Feed and Supplements
- ☐ Halter, Lead Rope, Lunge Line
- ☐ Back up Halter, Lead Rope, Lunge Line
- ☐ Tack and Back up Tack
- ☐ Tack Cleaning Supplies
- ☐ Wraps and Boots (regular and shipping)
- ☐ Cooler and/or Sheet
- ☐ Grooming Supplies and Towels
- ☐ Bath Supplies
- ☐ Fly Spray
- ☐ Braiding Kit and Scissors
- ☐ Lots of Treats

FOR THE RIDER

- ☐ Rider Health Card
- ☐ Human First Aid Kit
- ☐ Sunscreen and Sun Protection
- ☐ Water
- ☐ Helmet
- ☐ Show Clothes and Safety Vest
- ☐ Cover-up Clothes for Grooming
- ☐ Gloves
- ☐ Rain Gear
- ☐ Safety Pins, Sewing Kit, Spot Cleaner
- ☐ Folding Chairs
- ☐ Cell Phone and List of Emergency Numbers
- ☐ Watch

FOR THE TRAILER

- ☐ Safety Check
- ☐ Spare Tire and Jack
- ☐ Extra Ties
- ☐ Hay Nets and Hay
- ☐ Bedding
- ☐ Muck Bucket and Forks
- ☐ Duct Tape, Flashlight

FOR / FROM THE SHOW OFFICE

- ☐ Association Memberships
- ☐ Horse Passport
- ☐ Registration Papers
- ☐ Negative Coggins and/or Other Required Health Documentation
- ☐ Rulebook
- ☐ Cash or Chequebook
- ☐ Copy of Tests, Patterns and Class Lists

"Many people have sighed for the 'good old days' and regretted the 'passing of the horse,' but today, when only those who like horses own them, it is a far better time for horses."
C.W. ANDERSON

Show Log

DATE	VENUE / SERIES	JUDGE	CLASS	PLACING	NUMBER IN CLASS	POINTS

Show Log

DATE	VENUE / SERIES	JUDGE	CLASS	PLACING	NUMBER IN CLASS	POINTS

NOTES

"When you're young and you fall off a horse,
you may break something. When you're
my age, you splatter."
ROY ROGERS